Text: *Mark Richards*
Series editor: *Tony Bowerman*
Photographs: *Mark Richards, Steve Thompson/ www.sunstormphotography.com, Shutterstock, Dreamtime*

Design: *Carl Rogers*

Northern Eye Books

ISBN 978-1-908632-35-7

A CIP catalogue record for this book is available from the British Library.

Cover: *Muker meadows (Walk 4)*

Important Advice: The routes described in this book are undertaken at the reader's own risk. Walkers should take into account their level of fitness, wear suitable footwear and clothing, and carry food and water. It is also advisable to take the relevant OS map with you in case you get lost and leave the area covered by our maps.

Whilst every care has been taken to ensure the accuracy of the route directions, the publishers cannot accept responsibility for errors or omissions, or for changes in the details given. Nor can the publisher and copyright owners accept responsibility for any consequences arising from the use of this book.

If you find any inaccuracies in either the text or maps, please write or email us at the address below. Thank you.

First published in 2015 by
Northern Eye Books Limited
Northern Eye Books, Tattenhall, Cheshire CH3 9PX
Email: tony@northerneyebooks.com

For sales enquiries, please call 01928 723 744

'Linescape' artwork by Mark Richards
Inside cover: *Muker laithe barn*
Title page: *Loup Scar*

Follow Mark on Twitter: *@fellranger1*

 Twitter: @Northerneyeboo
@Top10walks

Contents

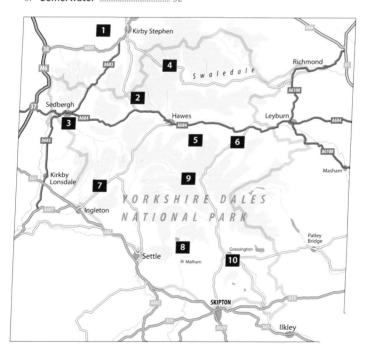

Pennine perfection

Designated in 1954, the **Yorkshire Dales** cover 1,762 square kilometres/680 square miles of the central Pennines. As well as some of Yorkshire's most magnificent landscapes, the National Park also includes a corner of Cumbria, where the secluded Howgill Fells loom over the River Lune. 'Dales' is something of a misnomer, for in addition to the beautiful dales the area incorporates great tracts of wild moorland, the famous 'Three Peaks' and an intriguing industrial heritage.

Over 1,300 miles of rights of way allow walkers to explore all facets of the Park. In addition, almost 110,000 hectares of open access land has opened up endless possibilities for exploring this heady mix of limestone and gritstone scenery. Upwards of 8 million visitors a year enjoy this striking countryside with its picturesque stone villages.

Swaledale barn in a hay meadow awash with buttercups

The Yorkshire Dales' best dales and valleys

The focus in the Yorkshire Dales tends to be on a trio of much-loved valleys: Swaledale, Wensleydale and Wharfedale. Yet, broadening the gaze, one finds other equally spellbinding valleys, such as Airedale, Ribblesdale, the Rawthey and Dentdale. To the north, the bounding valleys of the Eden and Lune stretch the beauty of the National Park into wider horizons of pastoral serenity.

Here are walks for quiet enjoyment and seasonal beauty, where nature still reigns amid traditional patterns of farming practice. Solid stone barns and field walls characterise the dale bottoms; and the flora of the dales is wonderfully diverse: many a meadow retains its native herbal mix — yielding a delightful aroma at haytime.

"When I am walking in the Dales, I am always conscious that I am walking not just through today, but through yesterday."

Mike Harding, *Sense of Place*

TOP 10 **Walks:** Dale and Valley Walks

THE EXQUISITE MAGIC AND SCENIC DIVERSITY of the Yorkshire Dales unfolds within this set of short excursions. Even in the more popular localities, such as Malham and Grassington, solitude may be found upon these gently trammelled, often off-beat ways. Try each and every one and be rewarded with a unique and enchanted view of this beautiful National Park, the scenic heart of the Pennines. Distinctive and beautiful, the Yorkshire Dales are quite unlike anywhere else.

Smardale   page 8

Hell Gill   page 14

Sedbergh   page 20

Muker   page 26

Semerwater page 32

West Burton page 36

Chapel-le-Dale page 42

Malham Moor page 48

Hubberholme page 52

Glasshington page 58

Smardalegill Viaduct spans the pretty limestone dale of Scandal Beck

Smardale

Superb valley scenery enjoyed from a trackbed trail with optional returns either in the valley or over open fell

What to expect:
Excellent walking; firm trackbed trail; pasture paths

Distance/time: 7km/ 4¼ miles. Allow 2¼ hours

Start: Smardale Gill National Nature Reserve parking off Beck Lane, next to the old station at Smardale

Grid ref: NY 739 083

Ordnance Survey Map: Explorer OL19 *Howgill Fells & Upper Eden Valley*

After the walk: Pubs and tearooms in Kirkby Stephen; two pubs in Ravenstonedale; two tearooms in Newbiggin-on-Lune

Walk outline

The main focus of this walk is the trackbed of the old Darlington-Tebay Railway. Thirty years after the line's closure in 1962, this level, all-user pedestrian excursion through the exceedingly scenic valley of Scandal Beck was opened with its great viaduct crossing mid-way. To make a round trip, one may either cut back from Smardale Bridge onto the viaduct from within the valley or, for pleasant contrast, come back over Smardale Fell, initially in the company of Wainwright's famous, long-distance Coast to Coast walk.

Smardale

In a landscape ripe with the promise of good walking, the shy gorge threaded by Scandal Beck is especially worthy. The trail draws you into the Smardale Gill National Nature Reserve carefully managed by the Cumbria Wildlife Trust. The name Smardale is intriguing, referring to greasy butter, implying the pastures here were renowned for producing rich and creamy milk.

Along the old railway

Redstart

The Walk

1. Go through the gate by the information panel to walk west upon the trackbed trail. The adjacent 15th-century **Smardale Hall**, with its curious pointed round towers, is screened by native trees growing on the steep embankments. The trail leads on beneath the gated **Smardale Viaduct** arch of the Settle-Carlisle Railway. *This bridge was opened in 1875. Now within* **Demesne Wood**, *the trail gives startling views of the steep-sided valley with an abundance of limestone-loving plants lining the trackbed. The woodland itself is ancient coppice.*

2. The view opens further beneath the limestone scarp of **Witches Stride** and you duly arrive at a trail-side stile. *A post motif shows a rare white-clawed crayfish — present in the beck below.* This is where the optional valley return rejoins the track. Head on via the gate to cross **Smardalegill Viaduct**, *one of a set of impressive age-of-steam viaducts in the area cared for by the Northern Viaducts Trust. Although constructed for two tracks, only one ever crossed this 14-arch structure.* A gate at the far end brings the walk onto a turf track which runs

on past a mighty double kiln limestone burner. *This produced lime not only for the railway construction mortar, but for steelworks in Barrow and Darlington, although it ceased working before the end of the 19th century.* After a gate, pass a lone, boarded up cottage to walk under a bridge.

3. Heed the waymarking guiding you immediately left up by the wildflower motif post to a stile near the end of the bridge. The long-distance **Coast to Coast Path** is joined here.

Ancient arch: *A cobbled drove road leads over lovely, gated Smardale Bridge*

Wainwright's guide to the route, published in 1973, came in response to his disappointment in the Pennine Way. It was indeed an inspired concept. The route has brought pleasure to many hundreds of thousands of walkers in the intervening years and no little economic benefit to the otherwise quiet surrounding countryside.

Attention is now drawn into the valley with the distinctive corrugations of medieval cultivation terracing — or strip lynchets

— strikingly obvious in the pasture to the right of **Smardale Bridge**. The open bridleway leads right down to the bedrock approach to this gated bridge. Head up the track beyond, rising beside the lefthand wall to reach a fence-stile.

4. This is a point of decision. You may relish crossing the stile (sign 'permissive path Smardale Viaduct') and following the dale-side path running north under an **old sandstone quarry** and evidence of pillow mounds. *(Locally known as giant's graves, they probably were used to dry bracken.)* Following the contours,

Limestone power: *The disused viaduct dominates Smardale Gill National Nature Reserve*

the path reconnects with the trackbed trail at the stile on the northern tip of Smardalegill Viaduct where you retrace familiar ground along the former railway.

Alternatively, to elevate your experience of this magnificent landscape, continue with the loose stony path of the Coast to Coast (sign 'Smardale Fell'). After a gate, the green track slants leftward, gradually gaining height onto **Smardale Fell**.

5. After a gate, keep right of the curious narrow walled enclosure. Where the path splits, either option will do, as they come back together to reach a four-way bridleway signpost by the wall.

6. Keep close to the left-hand wall, signed 'Smardale'. This grass trod leads to a gate — with a notice advising wayward C2C walkers to follow the wall right. You, however, go through the gate and head on down to a fence-gate. Walk down a track by **Beck Wood** to a gate and into the confines of the hamlet of **Smardale**. The route now joins the roadway known as **Towngate**, going under the **Settle-Carlisle Railway** to pass the rambling farm buildings of **Smardale Hall**.

The grand farmhouse is very old and the pointed towers infer Scottish baronial influence. At its core is a 14th-century tower house, added to in a courtyard form. There is also evidence of an earlier motte and ditch north of the hall.

Continue to the road junction and bear left to return to where the walk started, passing the excessively suburbanised station house, to complete the walk. ♦

Species rich grassland

The comparatively thin limestone soils in the dale harbour a veritable delight of distinctive plants, including fragrant orchid, the startling magenta bloody cranesbill and low growing yellow-petalled rock rose. These, in turn, host delicate butterflies that dance and flit in the sun — species such as the common blue and dark green fritillary, which is actually a pale orange. Among the birds, look out for redstarts and pied flycatchers.

The deep and shadowy chasm of Hell Gill

Hell Gill

A wander across quiet farmland with a wonderfully wild Dales outlook and a grand surround of high fells

What to expect:
Farm tracks; field paths, sometimes spongy underfoot

Distance/time: 8.5km/ 5¼ miles. Allow 3½ hours

Start/finish: Park on the verge next to the stone barn by Smithy Gill Bridge, north of Aisgill Moor Cottages

Grid ref: SD 775 965

Ordnance Survey Map: Explorer OL19 *Howgill Fells & Upper Eden Valley*

After the walk: Moorcock Inn at Garsdale Head

Walk outline

A farm track provides a simple approach via Hellgill Farm to join The High Way bridle track. The route then heads south by High Hall before slipping down the pasture bank to pass the former Youth Hostel at Shaws and visit the tiny retired kirk at Lunds. It goes over the youthful River Ure to cross the valley road and railway and runs back north beside the intake wall to complete the round.

River Eden

The only river in England to flow north from its birth, the Eden is blessed with a journey of exquisite beauty from its earliest moorland risings to the Solway Firth. As Hell Gill, it sneaks surreptitiously through a narrow cleft in the limestone before exuberantly leaping 8 metres over Hellgill Force. The young river then tumbles into the enigmatically named U-shaped glacial valley of Mallerstang, at a stroke travelling from Yorkshire into Cumbria. Passing Pendragon Castle, the river becomes ever more sedate. From Kirkby Stephen, it flows on by Appleby to Carlisle, consistently flanked to the east by the highest Pennine fells.

Lime kiln

Curlew

The Walk

1. Follow the road southeast, passing **Aisgill Moor Cottages** to turn left before the 'Welcome to Richmondshire', National Park and county boundary road signs. Go through the gate and over the **railway**, following the farm access track which swings left. As the track forks, take a moment to wander left with the path to view **Hellgill Force**, where the fell beck takes a considerable step down. *Passengers on the nearby Settle-Carlisle Railway get a more distant, fleeting glimpse of this impressive waterfall.* Walk back and, ignoring the fording track, maintain company with the farm-track wending upstream. Cross a gated bridge and go through two subsequent gates in passing **Hellgill Farm**. Continue on the green track up the pasture to cross a wall-stile next to a gate.

2. Turn right to cross the gated **Hellgill Bridge**. *Hell Gill Beck may be heard, but not seen, as it runs through* a deep, dark limestone cleft spanned by the high-parapeted bridge. Walk south along **The High Way**, simultaneously **Lady Anne's Way** and the **Pennine Bridleway**. *This section of path later crosses the national watershed of England.*

Where the path forks at **Jingling Hole**, keep left, following the acorn waymarking. You soon reach the intake wall and **ford** the source stream of the **River Ure**. *This flows through Wensleydale on course for the North Sea via the Humber Estuary, contrasting with the River Eden, which flows into the Irish Sea.*

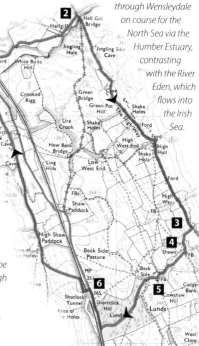

0   1km

1 mile

Hidden falls: *Hellgill Force tumbles dramatically over a limestone step*

Passing the **derelict High Hall**, advance by a tiny **lime-kiln at Grass Gill** to arrive at a track gate with a **High Abbotside** moorland regeneration scheme notice attached to it.

3. Do not go through the gate; instead go over the wall-stile to the right, descending the pasture into a groove leading down to a three-way footpath sign above **Shaws**. *Now a private house, this was the Garsdale Youth Hostel between 1949 and 1983.* Keep left

alongside the wall to a hand-gate and then descend the flight of stone steps to cross a **footbridge**.

4. Descend the pasture left of the power-line to a stile. After this, cross a **footbridge** to reach a hand-gate and then pass a **derelict farmhouse**. Exit via the stile and bear left to a flagstone bridge and wall-stile to reach **Lunds Church**.

Built in the mid-18th century, Lunds Church is long retired, yet kept in good order. See the Biblical quote on the interior wall — 'Cometh unto me and I will give

Fell barn: *Laithe on Aisgill moor, looking towards Yoadcomb Scar and Wild Boar Fell*

you rest'. There is still an 18th-century pew inside for those in need. In the former church-garth stand several gravestones. (The author's ancestors Brunskill and Metcalfe were buried here, carried over High Abbotside from Cotterdale.)

5. Head to the double-gates and enter the lane crossing the **footbridge** over the **River Ure**. Follow the access track up to the road, then the **B6259** right, rising up **Shortclick Hill** beside the curiously altered **Shotlock Tunnel**.

6. Over the brow, find a gate and fence-stile on the left, giving access to a track over the tunnel. Bear right, down with the wall, to a galvanised gate. Rise steadily up the pasture to merge with a faint lateral track among the rushes, aiming north towards the **farmstead**. A wooden field-gate provides access to a pasture. From here, walk through a gateway and then veer right of the ruinous farmhouse of **High Shaw Paddock**. Go through a gate attached to the sturdy stone barn to cross **Tongue Gill ford**.

7. The path becomes less evident, but keeps close company with the wall. After the first gate, walk through a

shallow 'borrow pit', *a colloquial term for the quarried source of the adjacent walling stone*. As the wall drifts slightly right, head on through the rushes to a gate and continue to a further gate with a considerable **sink hole** to the left. As the wall ends and a fence resumes, go through the hand-gate and quickly step over a roadside plank bridge before heading left to complete the walk. ♦

Black grouse country

Black grouse are increasingly rare, ground-loving native upland birds largely confined to moorland settings. The male's distinctive black plumage with purplish gloss sports a characteristic red sash over the eyes, the female is mainly greyish brown. In spring, males perform their lek (or mating) routine, in a communal lekking ground, a quietly removed open space. The term lek derives from the Norse 'to play'.

Tilted limestone strata on ther River Rawthey

Sedbergh

Riverside paths through pleasing pastoral countryside, looping back beneath the Howgill Fells

What to expect:
Riverside field paths; farm tracks; quiet roads

Distance/time: 9km/ 5½ miles. Allow 4 hours

Start: Joss Lane pay & display car park in the middle of Sedbergh

Grid ref: SD 659 922

Ordnance Survey Map: Explorer OL19 *Howgill Fells & Upper Eden Valley*

After the walk: Tearooms and pubs in Sedbergh

Walk outline

For all the allure of the fells, Sedbergh is blessed with enchanting valley walks. This is a charming encounter to enjoy in the summer sun when the meadows and woods are in full bloom. The walk strolls downstream beside the River Rawthey in harmony with the Dales Way, before breaking back up the pastures by Underwinder to join Howgill Lane and descend easily back into town.

Sedbergh

Until 1974, Sedbergh lay in the West Riding of Yorkshire, but a boundary change saw it switch allegiance to the new-made Cumbria. Visitors will adore its setting and lovers of literature its bookshops — it being England's 'Book Town' to match Hay-on-Wye in Wales and Wigtown in Scotland.

The town is renowned for its co-educational boarding school, with its long-established ethos of sporting endeavour that includes encouraging pupils to explore the backdrop Howgill hills. Will Carling, a former pupil who lodged in Winder House, went on to become the youngest captain of the England Rugby team at the age of 22, winning 72 caps between 1988 and 1996.

Sedbergh tea towel

Riverside path

The Walk

1. Pass down the steps by the **Dales and Lakes Book Centre**, and cross **Main Street** into the alley known as **The Folly**. Emerging from the arch, turn left along the footway to cross the zebra crossing and then turn right with **Vicarage Lane** – signposted 'Settlebeck or Millthrop'. At the foot of the hill, slip through the metal kissing-gate and rise to go through facing kissing-gates and walk on beside the wall of **Winder House**. Coming to a fork in the path, bear right via the gated wall-stile and traverse the pasture to a kissing-gate onto the road. Turn left, passing the **Akay sports ground**.

2. Coming close to the entrance to **Millthrop Mill**, turn right via the metal hand-gate — signposted 'Birks'. Traverse the meadow and, at another hand-gate, enter woodland, *pungent with wild garlic and bluebells in early summer*. Slip through the walled passage to bear left. Reaching the woodland edge, enter pasture at a kissing-gate. Pass on below a ruined gazebo, known as the **Pepper Pot**, and down through a gateway to a kissing-gate. The path now runs beside the sports ground's athletics track and adjacent to the **River Rawthey**. After a wicket-gate, rise up by **Birks House** to reach a hand gate giving access to **Birks Lane**.

3. Turn left and follow the road through the old **Birks Mill** community. Pass the food supply premises to join the narrow footpath beside an old **mill leat**. You'll quickly reach the **River Rawthey**, signposted 'Dales Way and Brigflatts'. (This 'Brigflatts' is the farm, not the Quaker Meeting House, which is not accessible off this path.) After a

Summer water: *Oaks and sycamores overhanging a stretch of the River Rawthey*

gate into a meadow, stay beside the river. A further gate and then a metal kissing-gate bring the walker to the point opposite the **watersmeet of the Dee**, Dentdale's river. After the next gate, the path straddles the embankment of an **old railway line** that ran from Ingleton to the still-functioning mainline at Lowgill.

You can see the **Brigflatts Friends' Meeting House** from the embankment, but it's better to make a special visit to it after the walk. *The name Brigflatts means 'bridge on a flat meadow', but there is no modern evidence of such a bridge.*

Looking left you peer down on a golf course. From the next gate, the path runs on beside the river. After a hand-gate at **Brigflatts Farm**, it becomes confined by fencing until a metal kissing-gate leads onto the **A683**.

4. Still in harmony with the **Dales Way**, we are obliged to follow the main road verge until, beyond the lodge entrance to **Ingmire Hall caravan park**, a footpath is signposted 'High Oaks' right

Swaledale view: *Drystone walls wind down the grassy sides of the Rawthey valley*

from a kissing-gate in the hedge. Follow the hedge to a plank and wicket-gate at **Haverah Beck** – *meaning 'oat hill stream'.* Slant half-left across the pasture to enter a very narrow, hedged lane and reach the little community of **High Oaks**. Pass through, via the hand-gates — signposted 'Lincoln's Inn Bridge' — and follow the subsequent **green lane**.

5. At the lane-end, go through the wicket-gate and follow the right-hand hedge, signposted 'L I Bridge'. Short of the fence, heed the fingerpost 'Luneside', guiding you half-left to a gate. Now on a **green track**, come to a gate and enter a green lane at the next gate, arriving at **Luneside Farm**. Thread through the buildings and, leaving the Dales Way, follow the access road. Pass **Prospect House** to reach the **A684** at **St Gregory's**, *a retired church kept in good order and deserving an interior inspection to admire the stained glass.*

6. Follow the main road right and take the first left up **Slacks Lane**. Turn right at the cattle-grid to follow the fenced roadway to **Underwinder**, en route crossing the **old Ingleton railway** again. Arriving at the farmstead,

go straight up between the barn conversion and barn. A stile leads into a rising pasture. Head up by a wicket-gate, passing some stately oaks to reach a stile into **Howgill Lane**. Go right, descending the winding road into **Sedbergh**. On meeting **Main Street** at the **Dalesman Country Inn**, go left to return to the Dales and Lakes Book Centre and the car park to complete the walk. ♦

Brigflatts Friends' Meeting House

This vernacular building is utterly delightful inside and out. It lies at the heart of what is often called '1652 Country', an area closely associated with the early years of George Fox's Religious Society of Friends. This Christian movement, also known as the Quakers, has included many business pioneers who have had a benevolent impact on society, bringing compassion into people's working environments and lives.

Swaledale's distinctive walled fields, stone barns and wildflower meadows

Muker

Two authentic vernacular villages are linked by parading first above and then alongside the lovely River Swale

What to expect:
Meadow and riverside paths; quiet roads

Distance/time: 10.5km/ 6½ miles. Allow 3¾ hours

Start: National Park pay & display car park, off Guning Lane, Muker

Grid ref: SD 910 978

Ordnance Survey Map: Explorer OL30 *Yorkshire Dales, Northern & Central areas*

After the walk: The Farmer's Arms and Village Teashop and Stores in Muker; Ghyllfoot Tearoom in Gunnerside

Walk outline

This is a walk of two distinct parts. An elevated daleside road is joined after an initial foray through the delightful Muker meadows. The quietest possible tarmac strip leads scenically to Gunnerside, with an option to cut the walk short via Ivelet Bridge. The return leg keeps to the low meadows, with their jealously guarded heritage herbage.

Swaledale

For all the Yorkshire Dales' scenic unity, no two Dales are alike. Swaledale is narrower than most, with lots to excite eager, questing eyes. Between Muker and Keld, the great 'island' hill of Kisdon is something of a physical curiosity, the valley road and river parting company here. At the end of the last Ice Age, a glacial moraine blocked the original River Swale, diverting it through the present eastern gorge. No doubt hugely influenced by the National Park, the farms and villages along the length of the dale's corridor have retained their vernacular integrity — and a wonderful greenness pervades every casual glance.

Muker

Swaledale sheep

The Walk

1. Cross **Muker Bridge**, straddling **Straw Beck**, to enter the village of **Muker**. Turn up by the **Literary Institute** with its ornate gable-end. The cul-de-sac road leads past **Swale Farm** to a footpath signposted 'Gunnerside & Keld'. The path becomes a flag-paved way that rounds a field barn and advances, via squeeze stiles with their own wicket-gates, through **hay meadows**.

The scent from the meadows, with their unique herbal blend, is intoxicating. No appreciation of Swaledale can be complete without at least once inhaling its sweet perfume. Seen at their best from late May to mid-July, these species-rich meadows are one of the most treasured floral wonders of the Dales, accorded SSSI status. The flagstone paving keeps walkers firmly off the grass.

Coming to the broad, boulder-strewn **River Swale**, turn right — signposted 'FP Gunnerside' — to cross the **Ramps Holme footbridge**.

2. Steps to the left lead onto a track, along which you turn right. The track becomes a metalled road but remains unenclosed. Ascending further, it provides a lovely outlook over the **Muker meadows**. *Its elevation enables walkers to gaze down on the twisting, stony course of the Swale and survey the many laithes, or barns, that seem to occupy every field. The road gives a wonderful sense of freedom with uninhibited views.*

Two miles into the walk, after passing under **Cock Crow Scar** and above **Calvert Houses**, attention is drawn to the Oxnop valley across the dale. The name means 'the valley where plough oxen were kept'. Today, **Swaledale** *looks totally pastoral, but there was a time when some of the land was tilled, with oats a predominate crop to feed the horses.*

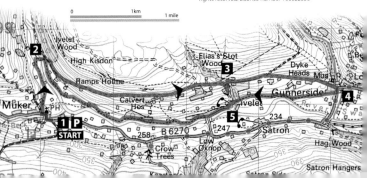

Summer bright: *Wildflowers flourish in Swaledale's rich limestone meadows*

3. Arriving at the junction above the **Ivelet Beck** re-entrant, you may cut the walk short, splicing it almost in two, by turning right, down to **Ivelet Bridge**. But the lure of Gunnerside's tearoom might be enough to hold your resolve to follow the full walk. In which case, keep left, crossing the road-bridge and cattle-grid in the dip. Rising from **Shoregill Head**, the road then sustains its scenic outlook as it drops gently into **Gunnerside**. (The Ghyllfoot Tearoom is beyond the Gunnerside Beck bridge.)

The village-name reflects Viking roots, composed of the Norse personal name 'Gunnar' and a reference to his 'summer shieling or home'.

Above the village and out of sight in the upper reaches of Gunnerside Gill are extensive remains of lead mines. Exploited principally during the 18th and 19th centuries, the scene is laid waste now, nature recovering the ground painfully slowly. The rich veins of lead (galena) were revealed by prospectors damming watercourses. When released, the resulting body of water would scour the slopes, forming grooved hillsides known as

Green shade: *The sun's last rays catch Swaledale's walled fields and slopes*

hushes. The term is an onomatopoeic representation of the whooshing sound of these sudden bursts of water. Now all is silent and a new hush prevails.

4. The walk departs Gunnerside by heading right from the green. The village road leads past the Methodist-maintained school at **Flatlands** to where the Ivelet footpath is indicated on a wicket-gate. A confined path emerges from the community into pasture at a squeeze stile. Traverse the fields by two stiles and a field-gate. After

the next squeeze stile, the path rises beside a fence above a river-eroded bank. Continue through a succession of squeeze stiles, passing behind a field-barn. Three wicket-gates on and the path dips through a dell over a **footbridge** and climbs into the hamlet of **Ivelet**.

5. Turn down the road to **Ivelet Bridge**, entering the meadow at the wicket gate before the bridge — signposted 'FP Muker'. The path starts beside the river but then heads straight on to a wall-top wicket-gate up from the water's edge. After that, it passes through hand gates to approach the river again. Coming

down a track ramp, cross the fence-stile and follow the river to the next squeeze stile. Path signs usher walkers across the next field and, by further wall stiles, past Ramps Holme. The ex-farmstead translates as 'the meadow where wild garlic grows', although there is no sign of this pungent plant today. The path leads on to re-cross Ramps Holme footbridge, from where you retrace your steps into Muker to complete the walk. ♦

Barns, or 'Laithes'

The first-time visitor to upper Swaledale will be taken by the sheer number of barns, liberally sprinkled in almost every walled field. Locals still call them by their traditional name: 'laithes'. They harmonise with the setting so beautifully, but their purpose was very down to earth: to provide a loft store of hay gathered in the immediate pasture and a ground floor shippon where cattle were tethered during the winter months.

A stone barn, or 'laithe', overlooking Semerwater and Addleborough

Semerwater

A unique marriage of the Lakes and the Dales in a stunningly beautiful cul-de-sac side valley of Wensleydale

What to expect:
Good, firm pasture paths; farm tracks; quiet byroad

Distance/time: 5.5km/ 3½ miles. Allow 2¼ hours

Start/finish: Low Blean's foreshore car park (pay & display)

Grid ref: SD 923 875

Ordnance Survey Map: Explorer OL30 *Yorkshire Dales, Northern & Central areas*

After the walk: Two tearooms, Raydale Preserves in Stalling Busk and Corn Mill in Bainbridge; Rose & Crown pub in Bainbridge

Walk outline

The walk replicates that shown on the information panel at the edge of the car park: it can't be bettered! It ventures, by the calming waters, to the retired Stalling Busk church and across the great lake's three feeder streams, to reach Marsett. From here, it heads back along Marsett Lane with its fine perspective on the valley.

Lake Semerwater

How often is this lovely sheet of water ascribed the appendage Lake? Literally translated, the tarn's name means 'Lake, lake, lake, lake'! 'Sae' is Old English for lake, to which the Middle English 'mere' was added and the later 'water' bolted on for good measure; and, as a vacuous modern quadruple flourish, Lake has been added to help anyone in any doubt on the matter. Other interesting derivations in the area include Low Blean or 'low rough ground' coming from the original meaning, 'rough cloth'; Stalling Busk or 'stallion's bush'; Marsett meaning 'summer-farm belonging to Maures' (from a diminutive nickname meaning 'ant') and River Bain or 'straight river'.

Stalling Busk Old Church

Waterlily

The Walk

1. First action: walk southeast along the road to pay your parking dues at **Low Blean Farm**. Now, clamber over the ladder-stile opposite the farm entrance — signposted 'FP Stalling Busk'. The meadow way leads, via two stiles, to an isolated barn and a stepped wall-stile.

2. More intimate with the lake now, the path runs on above the shore with an open view of the lovely spread of water lilies. *Locally known as brandy bottles, their yellow petals are a glorious sight in July. Semerwater is also home to the rare white-clawed crayfish.* After a gated wall-stile, the path crosses an open pasture slope looking down upon the alder carr marsh at the head of the lake. From a fence-stile,

continue beside a broken wall, past a set of wildlife interpretative panels to a gated wall-stile. Continue beside a wall to arrive at **Stalling Busk Old Church**, which closed its doors in 1909.

3. Passing through the gated wall-stile, you come to a footpath sign. You can follow the path up to **Stalling Busk** for its **tearoom**, reconnecting via **Busk Lane**. Otherwise, follow the path signed 'Marsett'. Passing through a squeeze stile, head down to the field-barn, slipping through by the gated wall-stile. Further stiles lead the walker across the pasture to find a stile to the right of a metal gate. Passing above a **roofless barn** and through further stiles, sneak through a gated stile close to another field-barn and continue with a wall on the right. A wicket-gate later allows you to switch to the other side on the wall and cross a **footbridge** spanning **Cragdale Water**.

4. Join the open track (the lower portion of Busk Lane) and advance towards the **cobbled ford** of **Raydale Beck**, slipping left over the **footbridge**. The path now joins a gated track, passing by the **Marsett Bothy**

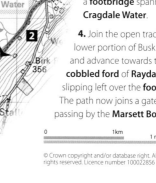

0   1km

1 mile

Water of life: *Semerwater is North Yorkshire's second largest lake after Malham Tarn*

barn-conversion — an independent hostel for the back-to-nature experience — before venturing on to the green in the farming hamlet of **Marsett**.

5. Cross the bridge with **Marsett Lane** heading northeast to pass above the grand **Carr End**. After one mile, watch for a footpath sign 'Semer Water Bridge' inviting you over a fence-stile on the right. Guided by **yellow-topped posts**, the path descends to a hand-gate and crosses a **ford**. It passes through an alder grove to a gate onto the road. Go right to return to the car park to complete the walk. ♦

Flooded village?

Local legend tells that beneath the 100-acre lake lie the remains of a village consumed by the waters in retribution for the inhabitants failing to offer food and water to an old man in need. He cast a curse on all bar one family, whose kindness was rewarded by being saved from the flood. The story is told in an old poem — The Ballad of Semerwater — by Sir William Watson.

A cluster of iconic stone barns in Waldendale

West Burton

Lovely pasture paths in quiet surroundings with an enchanting waterfall crescendo

What to expect:
Field paths; quiet roads

Distance/time: 11km/ 7 miles. Allow 4½ hours

Start/finish: West Burton

Grid ref: SE 016 865

Ordnance Survey Map: Explorer OL30 *Yorkshire Dales, Northern & Central areas*

After the walk: Fox & Hounds and the Village Shop and Tea Room in West Burton

Walk outline

Walden, the dale that time forgot... well, not completely. The walk traces up the east side of the valley before switching back to join the Whiterow Road down to Cote Bridge. It then loops back into the lower end of West Burton for a scenic surprise: the Cauldron Falls, the romantic inspiration for artists since at least William Turner.

Shy Waldendale

Burton is a beautiful little village, composed of 18th and 19th-century dwellings set deliciously about a generous Wensleydale green. The Saxon place-name West Burton means 'west defended farm', but there is no surviving evidence of a corresponding 'east defended farm'. These days, it is frequently called Burton-cum-Walden, due to the village's harmony with the side valley of Bishopdale. Walden means 'the valley of the Briton', native people having held their ground as Viking settlement took hold. The village grew as a small market centre with lead mining as its principal economic driver. This walk gives you every chance to absorb Walden's innate natural charm.

'Fox & Hounds', West Burton

Brown hare

The Walk

1. From the southern end of the **village green**, follow the narrow road signposted 'Walden only'. Keep left when this rises to a fork — signposted 'Walden South only'.

2. Before the last dip towards the river, cross a gated wall-stile on the right — signposted 'FB Cowstone Gill'. Here begins a fine succession of wall-stiles: the first gated, part-way along the left-hand field wall, the second with an attendant aerial! The path passes above woodland and keeps above the next wall. Don't be lured over the obvious wall-stile; instead, keep to the right of the wall. *See if you can spot the rabbit smoot — a hole through which rabbits and hares could pass (and also be trapped) — low in the wall midway along.* After the next squeeze stile, the path leads through bracken and the **Throsly Gill**, 'the mistle thrush's stream'. After the next wall-stile, the path continues with the wall to go through a flap-gated wall-stile and over a fence-stile.

3. Follow the fence left, keeping to the edge of the field and rising to a stile next to a wooden gate in the top corner. Descend to go through the wicket-gate, slip over the **plank**

footbridge and veer to the right of the old stone barns at **Cowstone Gill House**. A gated wall-stile puts you on course to skirt round the 'house' enclosure with a wooden sign, 'Walden Head', on the garden fence. Ignore the concrete access track; instead traverse the open field and go through a wooden

Valley high: *Walled fields and stone barns sprinkled across the sides of Waldendale*

field-gate. Now with a wall on the left and ignoring the wicket-gate part-way along, advance to **Hargill Farm**.

4. Pass to the right of the buildings and house access, dipping via a tiny red-painted gate into the dell. Hop over **Har Gill** to a gated wall-stile and up a short bank. Continue with a fence on the left, passing a stone barn to reach a fenced wall-stile. Traverse the next pasture via a further two stiles and two gateways to come above **Bridge End Farm**.

5. Turn left across the open track to find a hand-gate beside the wall-stile on the upstream-side of the house enclosure. Descend the bank below the house to cross the metal bridge spanning **Walden Beck**. Bear left to a stepped wall-stile into a meadow, finding a fence-stile ahead in the rushes. Now ascend the bank on a green trod, coming up to a metal field-gate. Go through this and bear left with the wall close by on the left. Go through a metal gate to pass the fascinating ruin of **Chapel Green** — but be careful of dangerous walls. The footpath goes

Hidden thunder: *Green water cascades over Cauldron Falls after heavy rain*

through two hand-gates, a squeeze stile and a metal hand-gate to pass a further ruined barn. The next gate leads into a drove, accessing the barns and farmhouse at **Whiterow**. Follow the lovely access track onto the road.

6. Keep forward with handsome dale views sustained, consistent with those experienced in the recent pasture path journey. The road comes down to **Cote Bridge**, with caravans dotted about the embowered beckside. Keep right, before the bridge, to follow the beck downstream. You'll come to wicket-gate in the meadow with a Biblical phrase on a wall-slate. You may like to cross the adjacent footbridge here, rising up the pasture to reconnect at a hand-gate with the Walden road, used at the beginning of the walk.

7. But far more exciting is the opportunity to discover **Walden Beck's** sensational dell. Continue on the path, rising to a gated wall-stile with memorial plaque. It goes over the ridge-top pasture by wall-stiles, passing **Riddings**. Going through a wicket-gate, pass a tank-spring and turn left where a fingerpost guides

you down to a further wicket-gate by a stone barn. The confined path leads down a passage with steps and into the dingle of **Walden Beck**. Cross the **stone footbridge** to wonder at the **Cauldron Falls**, an understandably popular place to sit and soak up the dingle's intimate beauties. The path leads straight up into **West Burton**, heading left up the broad green to complete the walk. ♦

Wensleydale Sheep

This blue-faced, hornless, long-wool breed was developed in the 19th century when the English Leicester was crossed with the Teeswater. It is one of the heaviest of the indigenous breeds, renowned for its versatility and striking persona. The dangling forelock of wool is known as its topping. The breeding produced hardy rams for crossing onto hill ewes. The quality and lustre of its curly wool was a further asset.

Rainwater eroded limestone pavement near Chapel-le-Dale

Chapel-le-Dale

Experience the quiet farmed essence of limestone country and the most modest of gradients in the lap of Whernside

Distance/time: 8.5km/ 5¼ miles. Allow 3 hours

Start: A lay-by northeast of the Hill Inn, along the B6255

Grid ref: SD 746 777

Ordnance Survey Map: Explorer OL2 Yorkshire Dales: *Southern & Western areas: Whernside, Ingleborough & Pen-y-ghent*

After the walk: Station Inn, Ribblehead and Hill Inn, Chapel-le-Dale; snack-bar at Philpin Farm on summer weekends

Walk outline

This walk tracks through a sumptuously rural limestone landscape in the open dale between Ingleborough and Whernside. It takes advantage of good farm tracks and very quiet roads, with two fascinating short footpath sections at the start of the route and near the end.

Limestone country

There is something magical about a landscape founded on mountain limestone. Geologists prefer the German term *karst* scenery. The weathered bedrock can be brilliant white when drenched in sunlight, whether in the form of pavements or low irregular crags. Surface water is seldom evident as a subterranean world exists, formed by the action of acidic rainwater dissolving the bedrock, enlarging cracks and forming passages and caves of great complexity. This walk immerses the walker in its every scenic trait — from potholes and caves to scar cliffs and surface streams running on the Silurian base of the overwhelmingly evident Great Scar Limestone. This is starkly evident with the furtive comings and goings of Winterscales Beck: now you see it, now you don't.

Boggard sculpture

Common rock rose

The Walk

1. Step back, as if towards the **Hill Inn**, but then go through the first gate on the left, signposted 'FP Ingleborough/BW Great Douk'. Follow the green track, the regular trod of Three Peakers intent on Ingleborough. Passing the **limekiln** head on the inviting track, go through two field-gates. Turn abruptly right — signposted 'FP Chapel-le-Dale' — following the wall down a **grooved way** which enters a dell behind the ruined barn of **Souther Scale**, which means 'the cobbler's barn'. Pass through the

gate and then the wall-gap to the left of the occupied farmhouse. Descend the bank by a gated wall-stile. At the foot of the succeeding slope, go through a second stile onto the main road.

2. Go straight over the road, crossing the summer-dry course of **Chapel Beck** and passing the lovely little church of **St Leonard's** in **Chapel-le-Dale**. *This is worthy of a few moments' admiration and contemplation.* Turn right with the walled road, rising above **Weathercote** to a fork in the way, en route rounding the sinister cavity of **Hurtle Pot**, thankfully protected by walls. Now on a track, keep to the right-hand way.

The intriguing statue of the Boggard of Hurtle Pot is the startlingly imaginative work of Charles l'Anson. The grotesque metalwork might not be to every passing walker's taste. Indeed, soon after it was first installed, someone tore it down and tossed it unceremoniously into Hurtle Pot!

3. The walled lane crosses a cattle-grid to pass **Gill Head** and, after a further cattle-grid, embarks on a winding course across the open moor of **Four Stones Rigg**. *There is clearly more than*

Quiet sanctuary: *Late 17th-century, Grade II Listed St Leonard's church, Chapel-le-Dale*

a quartet of limestone boulders in view, as well as the clint exposures. The name is likely to have alluded to either a 'lost' stone circle or tumulus.

4. The track comes to a **ford** at a right-hand bend, crossing a new cattle-grid into the environs of **Ellerbeck**. Pass to the right of the house, following the gated way as it swings delightfully along the pasture bank via a cattle-grid. The track approaches a wall and a low tree-shaded scar near a **stone barn**

with **cave** behind it. It then passes the farm buildings and 'retired' tractors at **Brunscar**. Now on a metalled road, stride on by a **tiny limekiln** where the Three Peak Walk crosses. From the hand-gate to the right of a small stone barn, continue on the footpath signposted 'BW Winterscales'. Traverse the pasture on a surfaced path to pass in front of **Broadrake**. *This retired farmstead provides accommodation and occasional refreshment for passing walkers and, novelly, blacksmithing skills courses, though one suspects most walkers will be content to forge ahead! The continuing*

Rocky bones: *Limestone pavement makes the perfect habitat for rare or unusual plants*

field-path leads through a succession of hand-gates to reach **Ivescar Farm**.

5. Head on northeast via gates with the metalled road, passing a low portal barn to cross a cattle-grid. *The pockmarked pasture on the right is actually limestone sink hollows.* Coming by a collection of **natural boulders**, turn right at a road junction. After a gate, the open road leads on down towards **Gunnerfleet**, beside **Winterscales Beck**. Unless, of course, you fancy breaking off to visit the **Station Inn** for lunch, do not

cross the bridge heading towards the Ribblehead Viaduct. Instead, keep with the open road, passing through two gates to cross the summer-dry Winterscales Beck and then through another gate.

6. Leave the open road by bearing right by the wall to a hand-gate up the pasture. Now with a wall on the left, stride on to come on to the 'suddenly dry' limestone bed of Winterscales Beck. You can see the beck briefly re-emerge beyond the metal trap-fence after the hand-gate. After the next hand-gate, bear left into the meadow, seeking another hand-gate in the dip where the

footpath becomes tightly confined. This can be muddy after rain; there is even the potential for a pool to negotiate en route to joining the metalled road from Brunscar. Follow the road left by **Philpin** **Farm**. On summer weekends, there is a snack bar here, a canny addition to the farm's frugal earnings. On reaching the **B6255**, turn left up by the **Hill Inn** to complete the walk. ♦

'Great Scar Limestone'
It's always hard to grasp geology, even when it's as starkly displayed as it is here. What you are witnessing is a sequence of ocean beds: the bodies of countless billions of crustaceans laid down 363-325 million years ago when this part of the planet lay south of the Equator. Plate tectonics explains how a rock now so solidly part of the Yorkshire landscape can still have it ancient origins many thousands of miles away.

Looking down from the lip of Malham Cove to the resurgence far below

Malham Moor

A compact figure-of-eight walk takes walkers to the brink of a dry Niagara and visits a placid tarn

What to expect:
Turf paths and open tracks; knobbly rocks and natural pavements

Distance/time: 7km/ 4¼ miles. Allow 2¼ hours

Start/finish: Car park close to where an open road crosses the outflow of Malham Tarn, above Water Sinks

Grid ref: SD 894 657

Ordnance Survey Map: Explorer OL2 Yorkshire Dales, *Southern & Western areas*

After the walk: In Malham village, The Buck Inn and Lister Arms, with The Old Barn and Beck Hall cafes

Walk outline

From the breezy wold of Prior Rakes we venture down Trougate to the brink of Malham Cove. For all the drama of its dale-foot aspect above Malham village — where the River Aire emerges with a strong resurgence — nothing beats standing on the clint pavement at the cliff edge, feeling the up-draughts on your cheeks, thoroughly aware you are standing in a mountain, not a lowland world. The walk turns up the remarkable dry valley of Watlowes to reach Water Sinks, confirming this as an upland 'dale' walk. A second loop visits the shores of Malham Tarn to swing back under Great Close Scar.

Malham Cove climbers

Dry Niagara

Malham Cove is England's silent Niagara. As the last Ice Age drew to a close some 18,000 years ago, meltwater stormed through the Watlowes valley from the vicinity of Malham Tarn, carving a canyon through a geological weakness. The body of water, sealed by permafrost from penetrating the bedrock, swept over the cove in a great arc reminiscent of the world's most spectacular waterfalls.

Rock dove, Malham

The Walk

1. From the car park, cross the road walking south to climb a ladder-stile. At a four-way fingerpost, head straight on, through a shallow hollow. A viewpoint cairn on the right-hand brow proves a worthy momentary lure, en route to a ladder-stile.

2. The path, here known as **Trougate**, wends gently down via a wall gap and over a second ladder-stile. Bear right at a path junction, with the exposed brink of **Malham Cove** close by on the left. **Extreme caution** *is required as the fall is unguarded.*

3. In the dale bottom, go through the hand-gate. Take the opportunity to step onto the **block pavement** on the west side of the cove-head and gaze down Airedale to the ancient field terracing above Malham village. Turn north, wandering with the dale-floor path beside the wall in **Watlowes**. *This sturdy structure marked the boundary of two neighbouring monastic estates: Bolton Abbey, in Wharfedale, and Fountains Abbey, in Wensleydale.* After the gated wall-stile, the path crosses boulders and enters a small amphitheatre. Clamber up the steps and pass to the right of a wall-end to cross a stile.

4. Heed the **Pennine Way** sign, directing you right on a contouring path that rounds the headland in impressively wild surroundings. Passing a vestige sheepfold, keep beside the wall to where the dry valley opens out to arrive at **Water Sinks**. This is the point at which the clear waters of Malham Tarn's outflow beck go subterranean. Seemingly dissolving as they strike the porous limestone, the waters are re-born and re-named the River Aire at the base of Malham Cove. The path drifts half-left, passing a fingerpost, to reach a kissing-gate beside the road. Go right to return to the car park.

5. Either as a separate stroll or as an extension to the first loop, walk north from the car

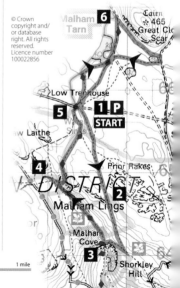

0   1km   1 mile

On the edge: *Dawn mists cover the dale below the lofty cliffs of Malham Cove*

park as directed by the Pennine Way fingerpost. Pass the outflow structure of **Malham Tarn** and a tree-shaded wall to reach an open 'white' road. Pass through the gate welcoming you to the '**Malham Tarn Estate'** and advance towards the shore of **Malham Tarn**.

6. Switch right upon a track running back under the cliff-line of **Great Close Scar**. This ultimately reaches an open track, where you bear right. Cross the **cattle-grid** and veer sharp right, following the wall back to the white road. Return to the car park on a lovely trail across the open pasture to complete the walk. ♦

Breeding peregrines

Peregrine falcons have been nesting at the sensational centre of Malham Cove for two decades, successfully rearing chicks each summer despite the peering eyes and close proximity of a multitude of casual visitors. While the choice of eyrie denies them the chance of anonymity, they are secure: their nesting place here is jealously guarded from rock-climbers. Their presence lends a timeless connection with wild Britain

Storm light illuminates the packhorse bridge at Yockenthwaite

Hubberholme

A walk of subtle contrasts, first wandering at ease with the Wharfe, then climbing to a seldom-seen elevated alp

What to expect:
Riverside meadows; dale-side pasture paths; open track

Distance/time: 8km/ 5 miles. Allow 2½ hours

Start/finish: Hubberholme Bridge

Grid ref: SD 926 783

Ordnance Survey Map: Explorer OL30 *Yorkshire Dales, Northern & Central areas*

After the walk: The George Inn, Hubberholme; White Lion in nearby Cray; Buck Inn, Village Café and West Winds Tea-room, in nearby Buckden

Walk outline

A merry meadow wander upstream watching the river dance from one rock step to another. Visit the beautiful farming hamlets of Yockenthwaite — from the Irish Viking 'Eogan's clearing' — and the self-explanatory Deepdale. Then loop back, figure-of-eight fashion, with the open road to climb easily onto the low wooded fellside shelf for an altogether delightfully contrasting view of the upper dale.

Upper Wharfedale

Above Hubberholme, Wharfedale narrows to a road, a river and the simplest of meadow straths. Inevitably, on sunny summer days, car-borne visitors coming over from Hawes via Fleet Moss and Oughtershaw are a steady procession, many halting by the open stretch of river to picnic and wet their feet in the rocky river. It's a great place for families to enjoy the liberty of the Dales; in truth it embodies the very essence of the National Park. Hubberholme itself marks a transition downdale as the valley broadens and native woodland flanks the daleside slopes, giving added richness to the diversity of the wildlife.

Upper Wharfedale sign

Bistort and barn

The Walk

1. To the right of the **church**, go through the gate as if towards the farmyard. Bear left off the track after the yard-gate, following the footpath signposted 'Dales Way FP Yockenthwaite'. This skirts behind the churchyard. The path is unambiguous as it crosses a stile and footbridge and passes a restored laithe (barn). After the next gate, stiles hold the walker to the field-edge and then the river's edge — with further field barns in view. A stile and then a gate lead the path up to a wall-stile beside sheep-handling pens at **Yockenthwaite**. A further hand-gate and field-gate bring the walk into the hamlet proper. *Most walkers laden with substantial rucksacks you meet are intent on the Dales Way, a popular valley-based long-distance walk*

that connects the Dales with the Lakes most beautifully.

2. Rise gently up from the open track, passing just below the farmhouse to find a three-way sign coy beneath a mature sycamore. You now have two choices: either follow the track up to the right, signposted to 'Cray', or delay — as this is the route we will follow later — and keep faith with the **Dales Way** for now.

3. Continuing on the Dales Way, advance via a gate past a long disused **limekiln**. After a second gateway, watch for the tight necklace of stones, *skeletal remains of an anciently robbed* **Bronze Age tumulus**. *This valley location is unusual as a tumulus would normally be set prominently on high ground. One must presume the valley was a major routeway in prehistoric times, this burial site of significance to people on journeys through the hills.* At the next gate, veer right by the galvanised fence gate to come up to a double wicket-gate. The path is guided right, rounding the top edge of

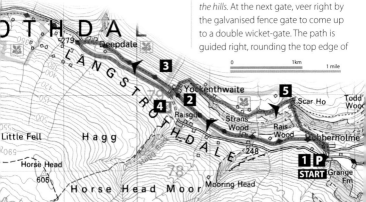

Little Linton: *Hubberhole huddles around its lovely old stone church and bridge*

the field, then down to a footbridge. It soon comes to a hand-gate and onto the track at **Deepdale**. Follow the track down to **Deepdale Bridge** and then follow the open road back downdale.

There are plenty of opportunities to consider the river's antics and its wildlife from the road. Dippers flit about, preying on aquatic invertebrates. In the river itself swim bullhead and crayfish. The roadside verges bloom with wildflowers. Look for aniseed-scented sweet cicely

and pink splashes of bistort. Summer sees blue meadow cranesbill, fragrant meadowsweet, yellow rattle, bird's eye primrose, blue moorgrass and carnivorous common butterwort

4. Once back at **Yockenthwaite**, cross the **gated packhorse bridge** to come up to the three-way sign passed earlier. Now follow the open track signposted 'Cray'. This rises above the **farmstead**, veering up short of the top house. Watch for the hand-gate to the right and a sign which draw the path off the rough track and onto the lightly wooded

Stone span: *The gated packhorse bridge over the River Wharfe at Yockenthwaite*

bank, enjoying handsome cross-valley views. A brief stumbly rise brings the path onto a limestone alp below the laithe (barn) known as **Little House**. Continue stepping over old enclosure walls, with hand-gates where a wall survives. This section of the walk passes above **Rais Wood**, *the term Rais meaning 'ancient cairn', possibly a reference to the ring of stones down by the river.* The path comes to a hand-gate and **stone bridge over Strans Gill**, a narrow ravine beneath your feet. The route winds on through the upper section of Rais Wood,

emerging at a gated wall-stile. Cross this and walk with a fence on the right, along the pasture alp and passing a curved bield. Go over a section of **clints** to pass through a field-gate and arrive at a three-way sign.

5. Take the 'Hubberholme' path on the right. This comes naturally down the bedrock track to **Scar House**, with its adjacent **Quaker graveyard**.

The datestone 1698 bears the initials of the Tennant family. The previous house was visited in 1652 by George Fox. The passion and conviction of his new vision of Protestantism deeply affected many who met him, including the receptive farmer

here. The insular life of a stoic dalesman gave a simple perspective on heaven and earth, eloquently revealed by Fox. This was the first property acquired by the Religious Society of Friends and is now owned by the National Trust.

The access track, concreted in the steep upper section, leads joyously back down into the valley to complete the walk. ♦

Hubberholme church

The 12th-century St Michael and All Angels' makes a beautiful contribution to upper Wharfedale. Indeed, the celebrated Yorkshire writer J B Priestley chose it as his final resting place. He described it as 'one of the smallest and pleasantest places in the world'. The church interior matches its exterior enchantment, furnished with Kilburn carpenter Robert Thompson's distinctive oak-carved pews and their signature mice motifs.

Sedber Lane, Grassington

Grassington

Soothing river scenery and charming villages amid a spacious, authentically Dales pastoral landscape

What to expect:
Riverside paths; field paths; narrow walled lanes; gentle gradients

Distance/time: 7km/ 5¼ miles. Allow 3 hours

Start/finish: National Park free car park at Linton Falls. If full, try the pay & display car park in Grassington. From Grassington, drop to Linton Falls from the the car park via Sedber Lane

Grid ref: SE 002 633

Ordnance Survey Map: Explorer OL2 Yorkshire Dales, Southern & Western areas

After the walk: Red Lion and village tearoom in Burnsall at the halfway point; choice of venues in Grassington

Walk outline

With Linton Falls as the exciting prelude, intimately observed from a suspension footbridge, wander serenely with the serpentine flow of the Wharfe to Burnsall Bridge. From here, either retrace your steps, or, seeking a sense of perspective on the greater valley setting, traverse the gracious pastureland to the south, via the enchanting little community of Thorpe in the bosom of the hills.

Grassington

Wharfedale has long been a gateway to the glories of the Dales for people with a Yorkshire mill-town perspective — with Grassington an immensely popular day-trip destination. The pastoral nature of the surrounding countryside is embodied in the village name, which means 'the grazing-farm'. There is also evidence of former tilled ground, with strip lynchet terracing of medieval origin, further affirmed by the nearby Saxon village-name of Threshfield, or 'place where corn is threshed'. It was in such places that most of the county's pre-Industrial Revolution population resided, deeply rooted in a productive agricultural economy, later dominated by arduous, but lucrative, lead mining.

Grassington village

Dipper

The Walk

1. From the car park, walk back to where the **Linton Falls** are signposted right by **Falls House**. Keep right again, by the millstream, avoiding **Little Emily's Bridge**, a quaint packhorse bridge situated on the former Threshfield-to-Linton-Church path. Cross the long **suspension footbridge**, admiring the weirs and the river bursting through the limestone bedrock on the Craven Fault.

This is the fourth bridge to occupy this site. The first, known as the Tin Bridge, was rather crudely constructed in 1814 to give access for workers to the mill. Spellbound by the acoustic agitation, linger as you will.

No doubt you'll not be alone: this place has drawn its admirers from long ages past, being the largest waterfall on the Wharfe. The hydraulic power of the water caused the National Park Authority to consider harnessing the century-old water gate as a hydroelectric plant.

Once across — at the foot of **Sedber Lane** — bear right by the wall-stile and traverse the meadow in harmony with the **Dales Way**, signposted 'Hebden & Burnsall'. The meadow route leads on by a squeeze stile and gated wall-stile, rising as a gravel pathway above the river to a stepped wall-stile. Here it enters a confined road.

2. Go right, passing **Brow Well fisheries** to where the lane ends at a hand-gate.

Over to the right are some **stepping stones**, *a very old crossing point installed for the exclusive benefit of parishioners attending Linton Church.*

The level pathway heads left via a footbridge and then goes through two further hand-gates more intimate with the free-flowing river.

Walkers only: *The picturesque pedestrian suspension bridge over the River Wharfe*

3. Cross the **suspension footbridge**; the adjacent stepping stones are tempting only when the river is truly low. After a hand-gate, advance to the next excitement: **Loup Scar**, where the river 'loops' beneath a picturesque limestone cliff. Rise and descend onto a walkway at the river's edge. Beyond a metal kissing-gate, the path leads to **Burnsall Bridge** beside the **Red Lion Inn**.

4 Follow the village road right. Rounding a right-hand bend, follow a confined footpath signposted off to the left after 30 metres. This traverses a series of narrow fields via a succession of wall-stiles with a green lane in the midst. Climbing a bank to a further wall-stile, come over the next pasture to cross a stony lane via facing gated wall-stiles.

5. The clear field-path dips through a **shallow gill**. After a wall-stile, advance with a wall on the right and then woodland to a hand-gate. After this, enter a walled green lane which ends at a gate onto a country road.

Green and pleasant land: *Burnsall village, its bridge and riverside sheep pastures*

6. Turn left, descending into **Thorpe** by the **Manor House**. Keep ahead, rising from the triangular green by some attractive dwellings to come to a T-junction. Turn left along the road, signposted 'Cycle route 688/unsuitable for HGVs'. This is **Thorpe Lane**, providing a grand view north across Wharfedale. Stride out along the road, traversing the northern slopes of **Elbolton**.

This 'hill of the fairies' is a pudding-shaped hill peppered with caves such as **Navvy Noodle Hole**. **Elbolton Cave**, *which has a narrow entry and an instant drop of 5 metres, was excavated in 1890 revealing the bones of bear, arctic fox, hare and reindeer. In 1920, Arthur Raistrick, the Dales landscape historian, revisited the cave and discovered human burials within stone cists of Late Neolithic and Early Bronze Age.*

7. Leave the road where a narrow walled lane departs right at a hand-gate signposted 'BW to B6160'. The lane winds its way down among the lynchet fields, ending at a hand-gate. Follow the remnant wall part-way down the pasture, slanting half-left to a gate. Then continue to the foot of the hill and a hand-gate onto the **B6160** road.

8. Turn right and walk along the road

for 15 metres. Then go left, through the gate. A clear path angles half-left via a wall-stile to cross the brow by a lone field-barn and then continues to a wall-stile. The path slips past the fixed gate in the corner to enter a short lane by Holme House. This leads onto a road, along which you turn left to return to the Linton Falls car park to complete the walk. ♦

Strip lynchets

Few pastures are ploughed today, but regular lynchet terracing — both up and across slopes — are the result of intensive cultivation from the age of strip farming. Each lynchet would've been horse-ploughed and crops hand-harvested to serve a large local population whose lives were focused on the ebb and flow of the agricultural year. The walk either side of Thorpe encounters these remains within what is now sheep and cattle pasture.

Useful Information

'Welcome to Yorkshire'
This comprehensive website draws together a wealth of information about visiting Yorkshire. **www.yorkshire.com**

Yorkshire Dales National Park
For in-depth information about the National Park, including 'What's on' listings of local events and tourist information. **www.yorkshiredales.org.uk**

Visitor Centres
Many towns in the area have Tourist Information Centres where staff will help with accommodation, heritage and outdoor activities. The main ones are listed here; there are also National Park Centres in some key locations.

Tourist Information Centres

Horton-in-Ribblesdale	01729 860333	horton@ytbtic.co.uk
Ingleton	01524 241049	ingleton@ytbtic.co.uk
Leyburn	01748 828747	ticleyburn@richmondshire.co.uk
Sedbergh	01539 620125	tic@sedbergh.org.uk
Settle	01729 825192	settle@ytbtic.co.uk
Skipton	01756 792809	skipton@ytbtic.co.uk

National Park Centres
Open daily April-October; limited in winter; closed in January

Aysgarth Falls	01969 662910	aysgarth@yorkshiredales.org.uk
Grassington	01756 751690	grassington@yorkshiredales.org.uk
Hawes	01969 666210	hawes@yorkshiredales.org.uk
Malham	01969 652380	malham@yorkshiredales.org.uk
Reeth	01748 884059	reeth@yorkshiredales.org.uk

Emergencies
If you have an accident whilst out walking and are immobilised, call 112 on your mobile 'phone, ask for the police, and tell them to contact mountain rescue. Be ready to tell the operator your exact location (nearest village, plus features named on the map close to your location) and the nature of your injury.

Weather
For the latest report for the Yorkshire Dales follow the link on the National Park website (see above) for 'Weather'. For details of local weather, go to **www. mylocalweather.org.uk** and click on the area you're interested in.